MY 1ST BOOK OF
CAMPING

Sara Kale

Rainbow Arts Studio
Copyright © 2023 Sara Kale
All rights reserved.

Amazon Page: amazon.com/author/sarakale
Email: sara.rainbowartsstudio@gmail.com
IG: rainbow_artsstudio

CAMPING

Camping is a super fun outdoor adventure. It's like a sleepover in nature. You can go camping in the woods, mountains, or even at the beach.

CAMPING GEAR

Camping gear is the stuff we need to camp safely and have fun. It includes things like a tent, sleeping bag, backpack, stove, cook set, food, water, first-aid kit, flashlight, map, compass and other essentials.

TYPES OF CAMPING

There are many types of camping, including tent camping, car camping, backpacking, RV camping, and more. Tent camping is the most popular of all.

CAMPSITE

A campsite is a place where we can set up a tent or camper to sleep in while camping. It's like a temporary home in the outdoors where we can have fun and explore nature.

CAMPSITE FUN

Campsites are a great place to explore nature, cook outdoors, and have fun with friends and family. We can also go for walks, play games, or just relax and enjoy the peace and quiet of nature.

CAMPFIRE MAGIC

Campfire magic is the feeling of warmth and togetherness that comes from sitting around a campfire with friends and family. It's a time to relax and enjoy the outdoors, roast marshmallows, tell stories, and make s'mores.

OUTDOOR COOKING

Outdoor cooking makes food taste yummy. You can enjoy tasty treats like S'mores, campfire hot dogs, burgers, pancakes, cheesy sandwiches, pizza, corn on the cob, popcorn, and grilled veggies.

SLEEPING UNDER THE STARS

Sleeping under the stars is like having a super magical sleepover in nature. You can gaze at the shiny stars, feel the cool breeze, and hear the sounds of nature like a soothing lullaby all around you.

CAMPING SAFETY

Safety first makes camping fun. Stay close to adults, have a camp buddy, be careful around fire, stay safe by water, use a flashlight at night, be gentle with animals, don't feed or chase them, and tell adults about any bumps or scrapes right away.

GOODBYE CAMP

As our camping adventure comes to an end, we say goodbye to nature with love. We leave no trace, cleaning up everything and being kind to plants and animals. Then, we go home happy and excited to come back again someday.

ACTIVITIES

Help the Girl get to the Camp

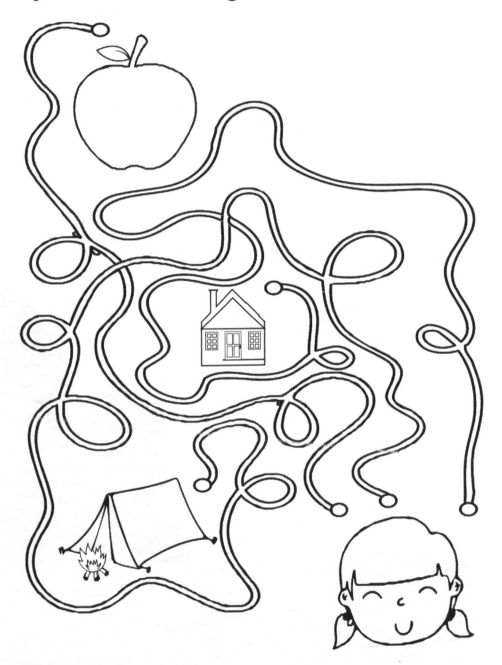

Camping Word Search

```
C D C V C H Q C O S G N T T N Q
Z U L H X N T B A N I M A L S E
K P D I T P V B Q Q A K H R C T
K C C Y I M F P A P M X N D Q X
B A V A C Q T O Q C E M V R B M
N M Z S B Q Y W S M K B N L J Q
Y P U B G I Z C V Z R P U E J G
G F P T O F N D K E S G A Q Q S
P I N D B O F M P S U E F C Y A
L R L Q F C T M X N Q H Z D K U
U E H Q J T A S T D G X T T B W
E T X X M C Y J Z X F C Z Y J J
I T C R Q C A M P W F U Y Z O N
E L X A D V E N T U R E B N F A
S B K V E U E T X A W H Z L L G
E Z R D V V Z K O B W X C J J Y
```

ADVENTURE   ANIMALS
BACKPACK   BOOTS
CABIN   CAMP
CAMPER   CAMPFIRE

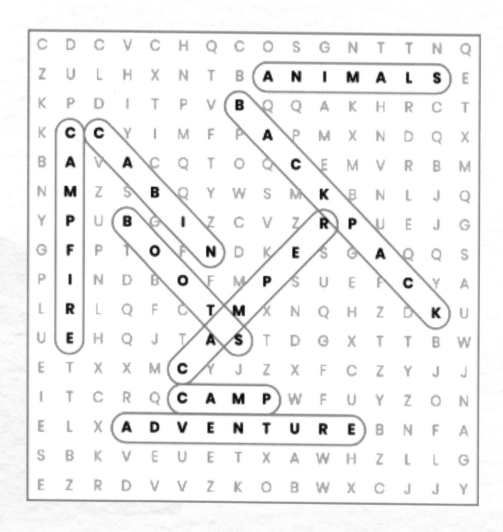

Printed in Great Britain
by Amazon

43000911R00018